CURSIVE HANDWRITING BEGINNER
Children's Reading & Writing Education Books

PROFESSOR GUSTO
EDUCATIONAL & INFORMATIVE BOOKS FOR CHILDREN
(PRE-K / K-12)

Trace the Cursive Letters
in the Alphabet and
then write your own.

Aa Aa

Aa Aa

Aa Aa

Aa Aa

Bb Bb

Bb Bb

Bb Bb

Bb Bb

Cc Cc

Cc Cc

Cc Cc

Cc Cc

Dd Dd

Dd Dd

Dd Dd

Dd Dd

$\mathscr{E}e$ $\mathscr{E}e$

$\mathscr{E}e$ $\mathscr{E}e$

$\mathscr{E}e$ $\mathscr{E}e$

$\mathscr{E}e$ $\mathscr{E}e$

$\mathscr{Ff}$ $\mathscr{Ff}$

$\mathscr{Ff}$ $\mathscr{Ff}$

$\mathscr{Ff}$ $\mathscr{Ff}$

$\mathscr{Ff}$ $\mathscr{Ff}$

Gg Gg

Gg Gg

Gg Gg

Gg Gg

Hh Hh

Hh Hh

Hh Hh

Hh Hh

ℓ̊i ℓ̊i

ℓ̊i ℓ̊i

ℓ̊i ℓ̊i

ℓ̊i ℓ̊i

Kk Kk

Kk Kk

Kk Kk

Kk Kk

$\mathcal{Ll} \quad \mathcal{Ll}$

$\mathcal{Ll} \quad \mathcal{Ll}$

$\mathcal{Ll} \quad \mathcal{Ll}$

$\mathcal{Ll} \quad \mathcal{Ll}$

Mm Mm

Mm Mm

Mm Mm

Mm Mm

Nn Nn

Nn Nn

Nn Nn

Nn Nn

Oo Oo

Oo Oo

Oo Oo

Oo Oo

Pp Pp

Pp Pp

Pp Pp

Pp Pp

Qq Qq

Qq Qq

Qq Qq

Qq Qq

Rr Rr

Rr Rr

Rr Rr

Rr Rr

Tt *Tt*

Tt *Tt*

Tt *Tt*

Tt *Tt*

Uu Uu

Uu Uu

Uu Uu

Uu Uu

$\mathcal{U}u$ $\mathcal{U}u$

$\mathcal{U}u$ $\mathcal{U}u$

$\mathcal{U}u$ $\mathcal{U}u$

$\mathcal{U}u$ $\mathcal{U}u$

Uu Uu

Uu Uu

Uu Uu

Uu Uu

$\mathcal{X}x$ $\mathcal{X}x$

$\mathcal{X}x$ $\mathcal{X}x$

$\mathcal{X}x$ $\mathcal{X}x$

$\mathcal{X}x$ $\mathcal{X}x$

Yy Yy

Yy Yy

Yy Yy

Yy Yy

Zz Zz

Zz Zz

Zz Zz

Zz Zz

Trace the words and
then write your own.

apple

add

baby

book

cat

cake

dog

doll

egg

fish

girl

hill

igloo

jelly

key

leg

map

nut

orange

pin

nose

sock

snake

tree

tent

uncle

vest

vase

wand

window

wasp

wood

yellow

yacht

zoo

zip

www.ingramcontent.com/pod-product-compliance
Lightning Source LLC
LaVergne TN
LVHW061321060426
835507LV00019B/2257